MONEY
AND THE LAW OF ATTRACTION

——— Celeste Byron ———

Copyrighted material
All rights reserved

INTRODUCTION

The Law of Attraction is a completely natural law that works just like any other law in the universe. It is a neutral law and it operates in the same way for every individual without exceptions, just like gravity. The Law of Attraction is very precise and infallible and it works regardless of whether you believe in it or not. Of course, it is better for you to believe in it and use it to work in your favour.

The people who are content to sit on the sofa and wait for their wishes to be fulfilled are the ones who are likely to claim this law does not work for them. But it only works if you take action to direct your personal energy and stay focused on the things that you want to manifest in your life. Most people are doing just the opposite.

There are many philosophers who have attempted to explain the Law of Attraction by comparing people's minds to magnets. They explain that our thoughts are like magnets and magnets do not try to attract things - they simply attract them without thinking or acting based on energy. That's the same way in which people are functioning – everything you have achieved, everything you have, everything that has happened so far and where you are was attracted by no one else but you.

People have a certain energy they put out when they have a thought and these thoughts attract things into their life. Every word has a certain vibration and the Law of Attraction (precise and infallible) returns things, persons and events that match the vibrations that you broadcast. So, the easiest way to live a happy and abundant life is to transmit positive vibes by staying focused on what you desire.

The way to supercharge the Law of Attraction is to write down on paper your desires and goals. Let's look at the proof. In a famous 1979 study, Harvard MBA graduate students were asked if they had set clear written goals for their futures. Only 3 percent of the students had written down their goals, while 13 percent had goals in their minds but hadn't written them down, and 84 percent had not defined any specific goals at all. Think for a moment which group you belong to.

After 10 years, the same group of students were interviewed and the conclusion of the study was totally astonishing. The 13 percent of the class who had goals, but did not write them down, earned twice the amount of the 84 percent who had no goals. However, the 3 percent who had written goals were earning, on average, TEN TIMES as much as the other 97 percent of the class COMBINED.

Once you start directing your focus by journaling your thoughts and desires around money, just see what shows up in your life - I think you will be pleasently surprised! The Law of Attraction - once understood and harnessed - can be your most valuable asset in life.

Now let's see how to use this personal journal to bring financial abundance into your life.

HOW TO USE THIS JOURNAL

The process used in this journal is designed to be simple and powerful. Every day you need to journal your thoughts on the following four key focus questions.

1. How much money do I want to attract in my life?
2. What will this money allow me to attain or achieve?
3. How will reaching my financial goals make me feel?
4. What can I contribute with the money once I have it?

Let's look at the questions in more detail:

1. How much money do I want to attract in my life?
If you don't know exactly what you want, you can't make it happen. To manifest something, you must know precisely what you desire. That means you must get very clear on the specifics, detailing the features as if your manifestation is tailor made for you.

'I'd like financial abundance' will not do. It's too vague for the universe to act on.

'I will receive an income of $60,000 a year. This will happen within three years' is much better. It specifies an amount, the timeframe in which to manifest and also asserts that you 'will receive' the amount and reinforces it with 'this will happen'.

2. What will this money allow me to attain or achieve?
Here you detail what the income goal stated in the previous question will allow you to bring into your life. Again, be specific. List the products, gifts and experiences you will finally be able to enjoy. Free your imagination and picture your desires in your mind as you write them down.

3. How will reaching my financial goals make me feel?

To supercharge the Law of Attraction, you need to add feeling and emotion behind your requests. Imagine the thoughts and feelings you will experience once you are financially free. List the emotions and take the time to experience them in your body - this turns you into a manifesting magnet! Examples include contentment, security, excitement, confidence, peace and gratitude.

4. What good can I contribute with the money once I have it?

The final way to add power to your request is to encompass a wider goal beyond just yourself. So use this section to detail how you can help a family member, friend, stranger who is in need or organisation in some way. The virtuous act of using a portion of your acquired wealth to do some good in the world resonates strongly with the universe. The old adage that 'when you give you receive more in return' is a universal truth known as the Law of Reciprocity. Use it to your advantage.

So there you have it. Do this four-part journaling everyday. This might seem repetitious - but that's the very point of the journal. You are reinforcing daily your wants and desires and it is through repetition and consistency that you will start getting what you want out of life.

This journal contains enough pages to cover three months - which is a great start and will begin yielding you results. Once you have completed all the pages, continue your journaling to build on what you have already achieved until your desires are manifested in full. If you know someone who is in need, please consider gifting them this journal so they can also begin their journey to abundance.

May the universe provide you health, wealth and happiness.

Celeste Byron

Date: / /

How much money do I want to attract in my life?

What will this money allow me to attain or achieve?

How will reaching my financial goals make me feel?

What can I contribute with the money once I have it?

Date: /   /

How much money do I want to attract in my life?

What will this money allow me to attain or achieve?

How will reaching my financial goals make me feel?

What can I contribute with the money once I have it?

Date: /   /

How much money do I want to attract in my life?

What will this money allow me to attain or achieve?

How will reaching my financial goals make me feel?

What can I contribute with the money once I have it?

Date: / /

How much money do I want to attract in my life?

What will this money allow me to attain or achieve?

How will reaching my financial goals make me feel?

What can I contribute with the money once I have it?

Date: / /

How much money do I want to attract in my life?

What will this money allow me to attain or achieve?

How will reaching my financial goals make me feel?

What can I contribute with the money once I have it?

Date: / /

How much money do I want to attract in my life?

What will this money allow me to attain or achieve?

How will reaching my financial goals make me feel?

What can I contribute with the money once I have it?

Date: ___ / ___ / ___

How much money do I want to attract in my life?

What will this money allow me to attain or achieve?

How will reaching my financial goals make me feel?

What can I contribute with the money once I have it?

Date: / /

How much money do I want to attract in my life?

What will this money allow me to attain or achieve?

How will reaching my financial goals make me feel?

What can I contribute with the money once I have it?

Date: / /

How much money do I want to attract in my life?

What will this money allow me to attain or achieve?

How will reaching my financial goals make me feel?

What can I contribute with the money once I have it?

Date: / /

How much money do I want to attract in my life?

What will this money allow me to attain or achieve?

How will reaching my financial goals make me feel?

What can I contribute with the money once I have it?

Date: / /

How much money do I want to attract in my life?

What will this money allow me to attain or achieve?

How will reaching my financial goals make me feel?

What can I contribute with the money once I have it?

Date: / /

How much money do I want to attract in my life?

What will this money allow me to attain or achieve?

How will reaching my financial goals make me feel?

What can I contribute with the money once I have it?

Date: /   /

How much money do I want to attract in my life?

What will this money allow me to attain or achieve?

How will reaching my financial goals make me feel?

What can I contribute with the money once I have it?

Date: /   /

How much money do I want to attract in my life?

What will this money allow me to attain or achieve?

How will reaching my financial goals make me feel?

What can I contribute with the money once I have it?

Date: / /

How much money do I want to attract in my life?

What will this money allow me to attain or achieve?

How will reaching my financial goals make me feel?

What can I contribute with the money once I have it?

Date: /   /

How much money do I want to attract in my life?

What will this money allow me to attain or achieve?

How will reaching my financial goals make me feel?

What can I contribute with the money once I have it?

Date: / /

How much money do I want to attract in my life?

What will this money allow me to attain or achieve?

How will reaching my financial goals make me feel?

What can I contribute with the money once I have it?

Date: /   /

How much money do I want to attract in my life?

What will this money allow me to attain or achieve?

How will reaching my financial goals make me feel?

What can I contribute with the money once I have it?

Date: /   /

How much money do I want to attract in my life?

What will this money allow me to attain or achieve?

How will reaching my financial goals make me feel?

What can I contribute with the money once I have it?

Date: / /

How much money do I want to attract in my life?

What will this money allow me to attain or achieve?

How will reaching my financial goals make me feel?

What can I contribute with the money once I have it?

Date: /   /

How much money do I want to attract in my life?

What will this money allow me to attain or achieve?

How will reaching my financial goals make me feel?

What can I contribute with the money once I have it?

Date: / /

How much money do I want to attract in my life?

What will this money allow me to attain or achieve?

How will reaching my financial goals make me feel?

What can I contribute with the money once I have it?

Date: / /

How much money do I want to attract in my life?

What will this money allow me to attain or achieve?

How will reaching my financial goals make me feel?

What can I contribute with the money once I have it?

Date: /   /

How much money do I want to attract in my life?

What will this money allow me to attain or achieve?

How will reaching my financial goals make me feel?

What can I contribute with the money once I have it?

Date: / /

How much money do I want to attract in my life?

What will this money allow me to attain or achieve?

How will reaching my financial goals make me feel?

What can I contribute with the money once I have it?

Date: / /

How much money do I want to attract in my life?

What will this money allow me to attain or achieve?

How will reaching my financial goals make me feel?

What can I contribute with the money once I have it?

Date: / /

How much money do I want to attract in my life?

What will this money allow me to attain or achieve?

How will reaching my financial goals make me feel?

What can I contribute with the money once I have it?

Date: / /

How much money do I want to attract in my life?

What will this money allow me to attain or achieve?

How will reaching my financial goals make me feel?

What can I contribute with the money once I have it?

Date: /   /

How much money do I want to attract in my life?

What will this money allow me to attain or achieve?

How will reaching my financial goals make me feel?

What can I contribute with the money once I have it?

Date: / /

How much money do I want to attract in my life?

What will this money allow me to attain or achieve?

How will reaching my financial goals make me feel?

What can I contribute with the money once I have it?

Date: /   /

How much money do I want to attract in my life?

What will this money allow me to attain or achieve?

How will reaching my financial goals make me feel?

What can I contribute with the money once I have it?

Date: / /

How much money do I want to attract in my life?

What will this money allow me to attain or achieve?

How will reaching my financial goals make me feel?

What can I contribute with the money once I have it?

Date: /   /

How much money do I want to attract in my life?

What will this money allow me to attain or achieve?

How will reaching my financial goals make me feel?

What can I contribute with the money once I have it?

Date: / /

How much money do I want to attract in my life?

What will this money allow me to attain or achieve?

How will reaching my financial goals make me feel?

What can I contribute with the money once I have it?

Date: /   /

How much money do I want to attract in my life?

What will this money allow me to attain or achieve?

How will reaching my financial goals make me feel?

What can I contribute with the money once I have it?

Date: /   /

How much money do I want to attract in my life?

What will this money allow me to attain or achieve?

How will reaching my financial goals make me feel?

What can I contribute with the money once I have it?

Date: / /

How much money do I want to attract in my life?

What will this money allow me to attain or achieve?

How will reaching my financial goals make me feel?

What can I contribute with the money once I have it?

Date: / /

How much money do I want to attract in my life?

What will this money allow me to attain or achieve?

How will reaching my financial goals make me feel?

What can I contribute with the money once I have it?

Date: /   /

How much money do I want to attract in my life?

What will this money allow me to attain or achieve?

How will reaching my financial goals make me feel?

What can I contribute with the money once I have it?

Date: /   /

How much money do I want to attract in my life?

What will this money allow me to attain or achieve?

How will reaching my financial goals make me feel?

What can I contribute with the money once I have it?

Date: / /

How much money do I want to attract in my life?

What will this money allow me to attain or achieve?

How will reaching my financial goals make me feel?

What can I contribute with the money once I have it?

Date: /   /

How much money do I want to attract in my life?

What will this money allow me to attain or achieve?

How will reaching my financial goals make me feel?

What can I contribute with the money once I have it?

Date: ___/___/___

How much money do I want to attract in my life?

What will this money allow me to attain or achieve?

How will reaching my financial goals make me feel?

What can I contribute with the money once I have it?

Date: /   /

How much money do I want to attract in my life?

What will this money allow me to attain or achieve?

How will reaching my financial goals make me feel?

What can I contribute with the money once I have it?

Date: / /

How much money do I want to attract in my life?

What will this money allow me to attain or achieve?

How will reaching my financial goals make me feel?

What can I contribute with the money once I have it?

Date: /   /

How much money do I want to attract in my life?

What will this money allow me to attain or achieve?

How will reaching my financial goals make me feel?

What can I contribute with the money once I have it?

Date: /   /

How much money do I want to attract in my life?

What will this money allow me to attain or achieve?

How will reaching my financial goals make me feel?

What can I contribute with the money once I have it?

Date: / /

How much money do I want to attract in my life?

What will this money allow me to attain or achieve?

How will reaching my financial goals make me feel?

What can I contribute with the money once I have it?

Date:　　/　　/

How much money do I want to attract in my life?

What will this money allow me to attain or achieve?

How will reaching my financial goals make me feel?

What can I contribute with the money once I have it?

Date: /   /

How much money do I want to attract in my life?

What will this money allow me to attain or achieve?

How will reaching my financial goals make me feel?

What can I contribute with the money once I have it?

Date: / /

How much money do I want to attract in my life?

What will this money allow me to attain or achieve?

How will reaching my financial goals make me feel?

What can I contribute with the money once I have it?

Date: / /

How much money do I want to attract in my life?

What will this money allow me to attain or achieve?

How will reaching my financial goals make me feel?

What can I contribute with the money once I have it?

Date: /   /

How much money do I want to attract in my life?

What will this money allow me to attain or achieve?

How will reaching my financial goals make me feel?

What can I contribute with the money once I have it?

Date: /   /

How much money do I want to attract in my life?

What will this money allow me to attain or achieve?

How will reaching my financial goals make me feel?

What can I contribute with the money once I have it?

Date: / /

How much money do I want to attract in my life?

What will this money allow me to attain or achieve?

How will reaching my financial goals make me feel?

What can I contribute with the money once I have it?

Date: /   /

How much money do I want to attract in my life?

What will this money allow me to attain or achieve?

How will reaching my financial goals make me feel?

What can I contribute with the money once I have it?

Date: __ / __ / __

How much money do I want to attract in my life?

What will this money allow me to attain or achieve?

How will reaching my financial goals make me feel?

What can I contribute with the money once I have it?

Date: /   /

How much money do I want to attract in my life?

What will this money allow me to attain or achieve?

How will reaching my financial goals make me feel?

What can I contribute with the money once I have it?

Date: /   /

How much money do I want to attract in my life?

What will this money allow me to attain or achieve?

How will reaching my financial goals make me feel?

What can I contribute with the money once I have it?

Date: /   /

How much money do I want to attract in my life?

What will this money allow me to attain or achieve?

How will reaching my financial goals make me feel?

What can I contribute with the money once I have it?

Date: /   /

How much money do I want to attract in my life?

What will this money allow me to attain or achieve?

How will reaching my financial goals make me feel?

What can I contribute with the money once I have it?

Date: /   /

How much money do I want to attract in my life?

What will this money allow me to attain or achieve?

How will reaching my financial goals make me feel?

What can I contribute with the money once I have it?

Date: /   /

How much money do I want to attract in my life?

What will this money allow me to attain or achieve?

How will reaching my financial goals make me feel?

What can I contribute with the money once I have it?

Date: / /

How much money do I want to attract in my life?

What will this money allow me to attain or achieve?

How will reaching my financial goals make me feel?

What can I contribute with the money once I have it?

Date: / /

How much money do I want to attract in my life?

What will this money allow me to attain or achieve?

How will reaching my financial goals make me feel?

What can I contribute with the money once I have it?

Date: / /

How much money do I want to attract in my life?

What will this money allow me to attain or achieve?

How will reaching my financial goals make me feel?

What can I contribute with the money once I have it?

Date: /   /

How much money do I want to attract in my life?

What will this money allow me to attain or achieve?

How will reaching my financial goals make me feel?

What can I contribute with the money once I have it?

Date: /   /

How much money do I want to attract in my life?

What will this money allow me to attain or achieve?

How will reaching my financial goals make me feel?

What can I contribute with the money once I have it?

Date: / /

How much money do I want to attract in my life?

What will this money allow me to attain or achieve?

How will reaching my financial goals make me feel?

What can I contribute with the money once I have it?

Date: / /

How much money do I want to attract in my life?

What will this money allow me to attain or achieve?

How will reaching my financial goals make me feel?

What can I contribute with the money once I have it?

Date: / /

How much money do I want to attract in my life?

What will this money allow me to attain or achieve?

How will reaching my financial goals make me feel?

What can I contribute with the money once I have it?

Date: / /

How much money do I want to attract in my life?

What will this money allow me to attain or achieve?

How will reaching my financial goals make me feel?

What can I contribute with the money once I have it?

Date: __ / __ / __

How much money do I want to attract in my life?

What will this money allow me to attain or achieve?

How will reaching my financial goals make me feel?

What can I contribute with the money once I have it?

Date: /   /

How much money do I want to attract in my life?

What will this money allow me to attain or achieve?

How will reaching my financial goals make me feel?

What can I contribute with the money once I have it?

Date: /   /

How much money do I want to attract in my life?

What will this money allow me to attain or achieve?

How will reaching my financial goals make me feel?

What can I contribute with the money once I have it?

Date: / /

How much money do I want to attract in my life?

What will this money allow me to attain or achieve?

How will reaching my financial goals make me feel?

What can I contribute with the money once I have it?

Date: /   /

How much money do I want to attract in my life?

What will this money allow me to attain or achieve?

How will reaching my financial goals make me feel?

What can I contribute with the money once I have it?

Date: / /

How much money do I want to attract in my life?

What will this money allow me to attain or achieve?

How will reaching my financial goals make me feel?

What can I contribute with the money once I have it?

Date: /   /

How much money do I want to attract in my life?

What will this money allow me to attain or achieve?

How will reaching my financial goals make me feel?

What can I contribute with the money once I have it?

Date: / /

How much money do I want to attract in my life?

What will this money allow me to attain or achieve?

How will reaching my financial goals make me feel?

What can I contribute with the money once I have it?

Date: / /

How much money do I want to attract in my life?

What will this money allow me to attain or achieve?

How will reaching my financial goals make me feel?

What can I contribute with the money once I have it?

Date: / /

How much money do I want to attract in my life?

What will this money allow me to attain or achieve?

How will reaching my financial goals make me feel?

What can I contribute with the money once I have it?

Date: / /

How much money do I want to attract in my life?

What will this money allow me to attain or achieve?

How will reaching my financial goals make me feel?

What can I contribute with the money once I have it?

Date: /   /

How much money do I want to attract in my life?

What will this money allow me to attain or achieve?

How will reaching my financial goals make me feel?

What can I contribute with the money once I have it?

Date: /   /

How much money do I want to attract in my life?

What will this money allow me to attain or achieve?

How will reaching my financial goals make me feel?

What can I contribute with the money once I have it?

Date: / /

How much money do I want to attract in my life?

What will this money allow me to attain or achieve?

How will reaching my financial goals make me feel?

What can I contribute with the money once I have it?

Date: /   /

How much money do I want to attract in my life?

What will this money allow me to attain or achieve?

How will reaching my financial goals make me feel?

What can I contribute with the money once I have it?

Date: /   /

How much money do I want to attract in my life?

What will this money allow me to attain or achieve?

How will reaching my financial goals make me feel?

What can I contribute with the money once I have it?

Date: / /

How much money do I want to attract in my life?

What will this money allow me to attain or achieve?

How will reaching my financial goals make me feel?

What can I contribute with the money once I have it?

Date: / /

How much money do I want to attract in my life?

What will this money allow me to attain or achieve?

How will reaching my financial goals make me feel?

What can I contribute with the money once I have it?

Date: /   /

How much money do I want to attract in my life?

What will this money allow me to attain or achieve?

How will reaching my financial goals make me feel?

What can I contribute with the money once I have it?

Date: /   /

How much money do I want to attract in my life?

What will this money allow me to attain or achieve?

How will reaching my financial goals make me feel?

What can I contribute with the money once I have it?

Date: /   /

How much money do I want to attract in my life?

What will this money allow me to attain or achieve?

How will reaching my financial goals make me feel?

What can I contribute with the money once I have it?

Date: /   /

How much money do I want to attract in my life?

What will this money allow me to attain or achieve?

How will reaching my financial goals make me feel?

What can I contribute with the money once I have it?

www.ingramcontent.com/pod-product-compliance
Lightning Source LLC
LaVergne TN
LVHW010340191224
799470LV00008B/300